50 Premium Flame Cooking Recipes

By: Kelly Johnson

Table of Contents

- Grilled Wagyu Steak
- Flame-Cooked Lobster Tail
- Charcoal-Seared Duck Breast
- Fire-Grilled Ribeye
- Cedar Plank Salmon
- Flame-Roasted Tomato Soup
- Charred Scallops with Lemon Butter
- Smoked Beef Brisket
- Charred Vegetable Skewers
- Grilled Lamb Chops with Rosemary
- Flame-Grilled Spicy Tuna Steaks
- Wood-Fired Pizza
- Grilled Bone-In Chicken Thighs
- Flame-Cooked Shrimp with Garlic
- Cedar-Planked Trout
- Grilled Octopus with Chilli
- Smoked Salmon Crostini

- Fire-Grilled Portobello Mushrooms
- BBQ Ribs with Bourbon Glaze
- Charred Sweet Potatoes with Honey
- Grilled Swordfish Steaks
- Fire-Roasted Red Peppers
- Charcoal-Grilled Branzino
- Cedar-Smoked Duck Breast
- Flame-Grilled Ahi Tuna
- Charred Brussels Sprouts with Bacon
- Grilled Steak Fajitas
- Spicy Grilled Chicken Skewers
- Flame-Roasted Garlic Butter Mushrooms
- Wood-Fired Grilled Corn on the Cob
- Grilled Pork Tenderloin with Mustard Sauce
- Flame-Cooked Paella
- Smoked Brisket Tacos
- Charbroiled Mahi-Mahi
- Fire-Grilled Rack of Lamb
- Charred Eggplant with Tahini

- Grilled Sirloin with Chimichurri Sauce
- Cedar Plank Grilled Shrimp
- Flame-Cooked Moussaka
- Smoked Chicken Wings with Spicy Rub
- Grilled Squid with Lemon and Herbs
- Fire-Grilled Bone Marrow
- Charred Halloumi Skewers
- Grilled Veal Chops with Rosemary Butter
- Smoked Salmon Salad
- Charred Sweet and Sour Chicken
- Fire-Roasted Beetroot Salad
- Flame-Grilled Brisket Sliders
- Grilled Duck with Orange Glaze
- Wood-Fired Baked Alaska

Grilled Wagyu Steak

Ingredients:

- 2 Wagyu beef steaks
- 1 tablespoon olive oil
- Salt and pepper to taste
- Fresh thyme (optional)

Instructions:

1. Preheat grill to medium-high heat.
2. Rub the steaks with olive oil and season with salt, pepper, and thyme.
3. Grill for 3–4 minutes per side for medium-rare, adjusting based on thickness.
4. Rest for 5 minutes before serving.

Flame-Cooked Lobster Tail

Ingredients:

- 2 lobster tails
- 2 tablespoons melted butter
- 1 teaspoon lemon juice
- 1/2 teaspoon garlic powder
- Salt and pepper to taste

Instructions:

1. Preheat grill to medium-high heat.
2. Cut the lobster tails in half lengthwise.
3. Brush with butter, lemon juice, garlic powder, salt, and pepper.
4. Grill for 5–7 minutes, until the meat is opaque and lightly charred.

Charcoal-Seared Duck Breast

Ingredients:

- 2 duck breasts
- Salt and pepper to taste
- 1 tablespoon olive oil

Instructions:

1. Preheat charcoal grill.
2. Score the skin of the duck breasts and season with salt and pepper.
3. Place the breasts skin-side down on the grill and cook for 5–6 minutes.
4. Flip and cook for an additional 3–4 minutes for medium-rare.
5. Rest for 5 minutes before slicing.

Fire-Grilled Ribeye

Ingredients:

- 2 ribeye steaks
- 1 tablespoon olive oil
- Salt and pepper to taste

Instructions:

1. Preheat grill to high heat.
2. Rub steaks with olive oil and season with salt and pepper.
3. Grill for 4–5 minutes per side for medium-rare, adjusting for thickness.
4. Let rest for 5 minutes before serving.

Cedar Plank Salmon

Ingredients:

- 2 salmon fillets
- 1 cedar plank, soaked in water for 1 hour
- 1 tablespoon olive oil
- 1 tablespoon lemon zest
- Salt and pepper to taste

Instructions:

1. Preheat grill to medium heat.
2. Rub salmon fillets with olive oil, lemon zest, salt, and pepper.
3. Place the fillets on the soaked cedar plank and grill for 12–15 minutes, until cooked through.
4. Serve with a drizzle of lemon juice.

Flame-Roasted Tomato Soup

Ingredients:

- 4 large tomatoes
- 1 onion, quartered
- 4 cloves garlic
- 2 tablespoons olive oil
- Salt and pepper to taste
- 4 cups vegetable broth

Instructions:

1. Roast tomatoes, onion, and garlic over medium heat on the grill until charred (about 10–12 minutes).
2. Blend roasted vegetables with olive oil, salt, pepper, and vegetable broth.
3. Simmer soup on the grill for 5 minutes, then serve.

Charred Scallops with Lemon Butter
Ingredients:

- 12 large scallops
- 2 tablespoons olive oil
- Salt and pepper to taste
- 1/4 cup melted butter
- 1 tablespoon lemon juice

Instructions:

1. Preheat grill to medium-high heat.
2. Toss scallops in olive oil, salt, and pepper.
3. Grill for 2–3 minutes per side, until lightly charred.
4. Drizzle with melted butter and lemon juice before serving.

Smoked Beef Brisket

Ingredients:

- 4–5 lb beef brisket
- 2 tablespoons olive oil
- 1/4 cup brown sugar
- 1/4 cup smoked paprika
- 1 tablespoon salt
- 1 tablespoon black pepper

Instructions:

1. Preheat smoker or grill to 225°F (107°C).
2. Rub brisket with olive oil and season with brown sugar, paprika, salt, and pepper.
3. Smoke for 6–8 hours, until tender.
4. Rest for 20 minutes before slicing.

Charred Vegetable Skewers

Ingredients:

- 1 zucchini, sliced
- 1 red bell pepper, cut into chunks
- 1 yellow onion, cut into chunks
- 8 cherry tomatoes
- 2 tablespoons olive oil
- Salt and pepper to taste
- Fresh herbs (optional)

Instructions:

1. Preheat grill to medium-high heat.
2. Thread vegetables onto skewers, alternating.
3. Drizzle with olive oil and season with salt and pepper.
4. Grill for 8–10 minutes, turning occasionally, until charred and tender.

Grilled Lamb Chops with Rosemary

Ingredients:

- 4 lamb chops
- 2 tablespoons olive oil
- 2 sprigs fresh rosemary, chopped
- 2 cloves garlic, minced
- Salt and pepper to taste

Instructions:

1. Preheat grill to high heat.
2. Rub lamb chops with olive oil, rosemary, garlic, salt, and pepper.
3. Grill for 4–5 minutes per side for medium-rare.
4. Rest for 5 minutes before serving.

Flame-Grilled Spicy Tuna Steaks

Ingredients:

- 2 tuna steaks
- 2 tablespoons olive oil
- 1 tablespoon soy sauce
- 1 teaspoon sriracha sauce
- 1 tablespoon lime juice
- Salt and pepper to taste

Instructions:

1. Preheat grill to high heat.
2. In a small bowl, mix olive oil, soy sauce, sriracha, lime juice, salt, and pepper.
3. Brush the tuna steaks with the marinade.
4. Grill for 2–3 minutes per side for rare, or longer for desired doneness.
5. Serve with lime wedges and fresh cilantro.

Wood-Fired Pizza

Ingredients:

- 1 pizza dough (store-bought or homemade)
- 1/2 cup pizza sauce
- 1 1/2 cups shredded mozzarella cheese
- Fresh basil leaves
- Olive oil for brushing

Instructions:

1. Preheat a wood-fired oven or grill with a pizza stone to 700°F (370°C).
2. Roll out the pizza dough on a floured surface.
3. Spread sauce on the dough, top with cheese, and add fresh basil.
4. Slide the pizza onto the stone and cook for 3–4 minutes, until the crust is golden.
5. Brush the edges with olive oil before serving.

Grilled Bone-In Chicken Thighs

Ingredients:

- 4 bone-in, skin-on chicken thighs
- 2 tablespoons olive oil
- 1 teaspoon paprika
- 1 teaspoon garlic powder
- Salt and pepper to taste

Instructions:

1. Preheat grill to medium heat.
2. Rub chicken thighs with olive oil, paprika, garlic powder, salt, and pepper.
3. Grill for 8–10 minutes per side, turning occasionally, until the internal temperature reaches 165°F (74°C).
4. Rest for 5 minutes before serving.

Flame-Cooked Shrimp with Garlic

Ingredients:

- 1 lb large shrimp, peeled and deveined
- 3 tablespoons olive oil
- 3 cloves garlic, minced
- 1 tablespoon lemon juice
- Salt and pepper to taste
- Fresh parsley for garnish

Instructions:

1. Preheat grill to medium-high heat.
2. Toss shrimp with olive oil, garlic, lemon juice, salt, and pepper.
3. Grill for 2–3 minutes per side until pink and cooked through.
4. Garnish with fresh parsley and serve.

Cedar-Planked Trout

Ingredients:

- 2 trout fillets
- 1 cedar plank, soaked in water for 1 hour
- 2 tablespoons olive oil
- 1 tablespoon lemon zest
- Salt and pepper to taste

Instructions:

1. Preheat grill to medium heat.
2. Rub the trout fillets with olive oil, lemon zest, salt, and pepper.
3. Place the trout on the soaked cedar plank.
4. Grill for 10–12 minutes, until the fish is flaky and cooked through.

Grilled Octopus with Chilli

Ingredients:

- 1 lb octopus, cleaned and tenderized
- 2 tablespoons olive oil
- 1 tablespoon chili flakes
- 1 tablespoon lemon juice
- Salt to taste

Instructions:

1. Preheat grill to medium-high heat.
2. Toss octopus with olive oil, chili flakes, lemon juice, and salt.
3. Grill for 4–5 minutes per side, until lightly charred and tender.
4. Serve with extra lemon wedges.

Smoked Salmon Crostini

Ingredients:

- 1 baguette, sliced into thin rounds
- 4 oz smoked salmon
- 2 oz cream cheese, softened
- 1 tablespoon fresh dill, chopped
- Lemon wedges for serving

Instructions:

1. Preheat grill to medium heat.
2. Toast baguette slices on the grill for 1–2 minutes per side until golden.
3. Spread cream cheese on each slice, top with smoked salmon, and garnish with dill.
4. Serve with a squeeze of lemon.

Fire-Grilled Portobello Mushrooms
 Ingredients:

- 4 large portobello mushrooms, stems removed
- 2 tablespoons olive oil
- 1 tablespoon balsamic vinegar
- 2 cloves garlic, minced
- Salt and pepper to taste

Instructions:

1. Preheat grill to medium heat.
2. Whisk together olive oil, balsamic vinegar, garlic, salt, and pepper.
3. Brush mushrooms with the marinade.
4. Grill for 4–5 minutes per side until tender and charred.

BBQ Ribs with Bourbon Glaze
Ingredients:

- 2 racks of baby back ribs
- 1/2 cup BBQ sauce
- 1/4 cup bourbon
- 2 tablespoons brown sugar
- 1 teaspoon smoked paprika
- Salt and pepper to taste

Instructions:

1. Preheat grill to low heat (about 250°F or 120°C).
2. Season ribs with salt, pepper, and smoked paprika.
3. Grill ribs for 2–3 hours, brushing with bourbon BBQ glaze every 30 minutes.
4. Finish grilling over higher heat for 5–10 minutes for a crispy finish.

Charred Sweet Potatoes with Honey

Ingredients:

- 4 medium sweet potatoes, peeled and sliced
- 2 tablespoons olive oil
- 1 tablespoon honey
- Salt and pepper to taste
- Fresh thyme (optional)

Instructions:

1. Preheat grill to medium-high heat.
2. Toss sweet potato slices with olive oil, honey, salt, and pepper.
3. Grill for 3–4 minutes per side, until tender and lightly charred.
4. Garnish with fresh thyme before serving.

Grilled Swordfish Steaks

Ingredients:

- 2 swordfish steaks
- 2 tablespoons olive oil
- 1 tablespoon lemon juice
- 1 teaspoon dried oregano
- Salt and pepper to taste

Instructions:

1. Preheat grill to medium-high heat.
2. Rub swordfish steaks with olive oil, lemon juice, oregano, salt, and pepper.
3. Grill for 3–4 minutes per side, until the fish is opaque and easily flakes.
4. Serve with a drizzle of fresh lemon juice.

Fire-Roasted Red Peppers

Ingredients:

- 4 red bell peppers
- Olive oil for drizzling
- Salt and pepper to taste

Instructions:

1. Preheat grill to high heat.
2. Place peppers directly on the grill and cook, turning occasionally, until the skins are charred and blistered (about 10–15 minutes).
3. Remove from heat and let cool slightly.
4. Peel off the skins, remove seeds, and drizzle with olive oil, salt, and pepper before serving.

Charcoal-Grilled Branzino

Ingredients:

- 2 whole branzino, cleaned and gutted
- 2 tablespoons olive oil
- 2 cloves garlic, minced
- 1 tablespoon fresh parsley, chopped
- Lemon wedges for serving
- Salt and pepper to taste

Instructions:

1. Preheat charcoal grill to medium-high heat.
2. Rub the branzino with olive oil, garlic, parsley, salt, and pepper.
3. Grill for 5–7 minutes per side, until the fish flakes easily.
4. Serve with lemon wedges and extra parsley.

Cedar-Smoked Duck Breast

Ingredients:

- 2 duck breasts
- 1 cedar plank, soaked for 1 hour
- 1 tablespoon olive oil
- Salt and pepper to taste
- 1 teaspoon honey

Instructions:

1. Preheat grill to medium heat.
2. Rub duck breasts with olive oil, salt, and pepper.
3. Place the duck on the soaked cedar plank and smoke for 12–15 minutes, until the skin is crisp and the duck is cooked to medium-rare.
4. Drizzle with honey before serving.

Flame-Grilled Ahi Tuna

Ingredients:

- 2 ahi tuna steaks
- 2 tablespoons sesame oil
- 1 tablespoon soy sauce
- 1 teaspoon wasabi paste
- Salt and pepper to taste

Instructions:

1. Preheat grill to high heat.
2. Rub tuna steaks with sesame oil, soy sauce, wasabi paste, salt, and pepper.
3. Grill for 1–2 minutes per side for rare, or longer for desired doneness.
4. Serve with a sprinkle of sesame seeds and a drizzle of soy sauce.

Charred Brussels Sprouts with Bacon

Ingredients:

- 1 lb Brussels sprouts, trimmed
- 4 slices bacon, chopped
- 1 tablespoon olive oil
- Salt and pepper to taste

Instructions:

1. Preheat grill to medium-high heat.
2. Toss Brussels sprouts with olive oil, salt, and pepper.
3. Grill for 8–10 minutes, turning occasionally, until charred and tender.
4. While grilling, cook bacon in a skillet until crispy.
5. Toss Brussels sprouts with bacon and serve.

Grilled Steak Fajitas

Ingredients:

- 1 lb flank steak
- 1 tablespoon olive oil
- 1 teaspoon chili powder
- 1 teaspoon cumin
- 1/2 teaspoon garlic powder
- 1 red bell pepper, sliced
- 1 yellow onion, sliced
- Tortillas for serving

Instructions:

1. Preheat grill to medium-high heat.
2. Rub the steak with olive oil, chili powder, cumin, garlic powder, salt, and pepper.
3. Grill the steak for 4–5 minutes per side, until medium-rare.
4. Grill bell pepper and onion slices for 3–4 minutes, until tender and charred.
5. Slice the steak thinly and serve with vegetables on warm tortillas.

Spicy Grilled Chicken Skewers

Ingredients:

- 1 lb chicken breast, cut into cubes
- 2 tablespoons olive oil
- 1 tablespoon sriracha sauce
- 1 tablespoon soy sauce
- 1 teaspoon smoked paprika
- 1 teaspoon garlic powder
- Salt and pepper to taste

Instructions:

1. Preheat grill to medium-high heat.
2. Toss chicken cubes with olive oil, sriracha, soy sauce, paprika, garlic powder, salt, and pepper.
3. Thread chicken onto skewers and grill for 4–5 minutes per side until fully cooked.
4. Serve with a drizzle of extra sriracha sauce.

Flame-Roasted Garlic Butter Mushrooms

Ingredients:

- 1 lb whole mushrooms
- 2 tablespoons unsalted butter, melted
- 3 cloves garlic, minced
- 1 tablespoon fresh parsley, chopped
- Salt and pepper to taste

Instructions:

1. Preheat grill to medium-high heat.
2. Toss mushrooms with melted butter, garlic, salt, and pepper.
3. Grill mushrooms for 4–5 minutes per side, until golden and tender.
4. Sprinkle with fresh parsley and serve.

Wood-Fired Grilled Corn on the Cob

Ingredients:

- 4 ears of corn, husked
- 2 tablespoons butter
- Salt and pepper to taste

Instructions:

1. Preheat grill to medium-high heat.
2. Place corn directly on the grill and cook, turning every 2–3 minutes, until the kernels are charred and tender (about 10 minutes).
3. Brush with butter and sprinkle with salt and pepper before serving.

Grilled Pork Tenderloin with Mustard Sauce
Ingredients:

- 1 pork tenderloin (about 1 lb)
- 2 tablespoons olive oil
- 1 tablespoon Dijon mustard
- 1 tablespoon honey
- 1 teaspoon garlic powder
- Salt and pepper to taste

Instructions:

1. Preheat grill to medium-high heat.
2. Rub the pork tenderloin with olive oil, mustard, honey, garlic powder, salt, and pepper.
3. Grill the pork for 4–5 minutes per side, until it reaches an internal temperature of 145°F (63°C).
4. Let the pork rest for 5 minutes before slicing and serving with a drizzle of mustard sauce.

Flame-Cooked Paella

Ingredients:

- 1 lb shrimp, peeled and deveined
- 1/2 lb chicken thighs, cut into pieces
- 1/2 lb chorizo, sliced
- 1 onion, chopped
- 1 bell pepper, chopped
- 2 cloves garlic, minced
- 1 1/2 cups short-grain rice
- 1/4 teaspoon saffron
- 3 cups chicken broth
- 1/2 cup peas
- Olive oil for cooking
- Salt and pepper to taste

Instructions:

1. Preheat grill to medium-high heat.
2. In a large paella pan, heat olive oil and cook chicken and chorizo until browned.
3. Add onion, bell pepper, and garlic; cook until softened.
4. Stir in rice and saffron, then pour in chicken broth.

5. Bring to a simmer, then cover and cook on the grill for 20 minutes, adding shrimp and peas halfway through.

6. Once rice is tender and liquid absorbed, serve hot.

Smoked Brisket Tacos

Ingredients:

- 1 lb beef brisket
- 1 tablespoon chili powder
- 1 teaspoon garlic powder
- 1 teaspoon paprika
- Salt and pepper to taste
- 1 tablespoon olive oil
- Small corn tortillas
- Toppings: chopped cilantro, diced onions, lime wedges

Instructions:

1. Preheat smoker to 225°F (107°C).
2. Rub brisket with chili powder, garlic powder, paprika, salt, and pepper.
3. Smoke the brisket for 6–8 hours, until tender and easily shredded.
4. Shred the brisket and serve in corn tortillas, topped with cilantro, onions, and a squeeze of lime.

Charbroiled Mahi-Mahi

Ingredients:

- 2 mahi-mahi fillets
- 2 tablespoons olive oil
- 1 teaspoon lemon zest
- 1 tablespoon lemon juice
- Salt and pepper to taste

Instructions:

1. Preheat grill to medium-high heat.
2. Rub mahi-mahi fillets with olive oil, lemon zest, lemon juice, salt, and pepper.
3. Grill for 3–4 minutes per side, until the fish is cooked through and flakes easily.
4. Serve with additional lemon wedges.

Fire-Grilled Rack of Lamb

Ingredients:

- 1 rack of lamb (8-10 ribs)
- 2 tablespoons olive oil
- 2 cloves garlic, minced
- 1 tablespoon fresh rosemary, chopped
- 1 tablespoon fresh thyme, chopped
- Salt and pepper to taste

Instructions:

1. Preheat grill to medium-high heat.
2. Rub the lamb with olive oil, garlic, rosemary, thyme, salt, and pepper.
3. Grill for 4–5 minutes per side, until the meat reaches desired doneness (about 120°F for medium-rare).
4. Let rest for 5 minutes before slicing and serving.

Charred Eggplant with Tahini

Ingredients:

- 2 medium eggplants, sliced into rounds
- 2 tablespoons olive oil
- 1 tablespoon lemon juice
- 1/2 cup tahini
- 1 garlic clove, minced
- Salt and pepper to taste
- Fresh parsley for garnish

Instructions:

1. Preheat grill to medium-high heat.
2. Brush eggplant slices with olive oil and season with salt and pepper.
3. Grill for 3–4 minutes per side, until charred and tender.
4. Whisk together tahini, lemon juice, garlic, salt, and pepper.
5. Drizzle tahini sauce over grilled eggplant and garnish with parsley.

Grilled Sirloin with Chimichurri Sauce

Ingredients:

- 2 sirloin steaks
- 2 tablespoons olive oil
- Salt and pepper to taste

For the chimichurri sauce:

- 1/2 cup fresh parsley, chopped
- 3 tablespoons red wine vinegar
- 2 cloves garlic, minced
- 1/4 teaspoon red pepper flakes
- 1/4 cup olive oil
- Salt to taste

Instructions:

1. Preheat grill to medium-high heat.
2. Rub steaks with olive oil, salt, and pepper.
3. Grill for 4–5 minutes per side for medium-rare, or longer for desired doneness.
4. To make chimichurri, combine parsley, vinegar, garlic, red pepper flakes, olive oil, and salt.
5. Serve steaks with chimichurri sauce on top.

Cedar Plank Grilled Shrimp

Ingredients:

- 1 lb large shrimp, peeled and deveined
- 1 cedar plank, soaked for 1 hour
- 2 tablespoons olive oil
- 1 tablespoon lemon juice
- 2 cloves garlic, minced
- Salt and pepper to taste

Instructions:

1. Preheat grill to medium heat.
2. Toss shrimp with olive oil, lemon juice, garlic, salt, and pepper.
3. Arrange shrimp on the soaked cedar plank.
4. Grill for 5–7 minutes, until shrimp are opaque and lightly charred.

Flame-Cooked Moussaka

Ingredients:

- 2 eggplants, sliced into rounds
- 1 lb ground lamb or beef
- 1 onion, chopped
- 2 cloves garlic, minced
- 1/2 cup red wine
- 1 can diced tomatoes
- 1/2 teaspoon cinnamon
- 1/4 teaspoon nutmeg
- 2 cups béchamel sauce (made with butter, flour, milk, and nutmeg)
- Olive oil for cooking
- Salt and pepper to taste

Instructions:

1. Preheat grill to medium-high heat.
2. Grill eggplant slices for 3–4 minutes per side until tender and charred.
3. In a pan, cook ground lamb with onion and garlic until browned. Add wine, tomatoes, cinnamon, nutmeg, salt, and pepper. Simmer for 10–15 minutes.
4. Layer grilled eggplant, meat mixture, and béchamel sauce in a baking dish.
5. Bake on the grill for 20–25 minutes until bubbly and golden. Let rest before serving.

Smoked Chicken Wings with Spicy Rub
Ingredients:

- 10–12 chicken wings
- 1 tablespoon olive oil
- 1 tablespoon smoked paprika
- 1 teaspoon cayenne pepper
- 1 teaspoon garlic powder
- 1 teaspoon onion powder
- Salt and pepper to taste
- 1 tablespoon honey (optional for a touch of sweetness)

Instructions:

1. Preheat smoker to 225°F (107°C).
2. Rub chicken wings with olive oil, smoked paprika, cayenne, garlic powder, onion powder, salt, and pepper.
3. Place wings in the smoker and cook for 2–3 hours, turning halfway, until the wings are tender and smoky.
4. Optionally, drizzle with honey during the last 10 minutes of smoking for extra flavor.
5. Serve with your favorite dipping sauce.

Grilled Squid with Lemon and Herbs

Ingredients:

- 1 lb fresh squid, cleaned and sliced into rings
- 2 tablespoons olive oil
- 1 tablespoon lemon juice
- 2 cloves garlic, minced
- 1 teaspoon fresh thyme leaves
- Salt and pepper to taste

Instructions:

1. Preheat grill to medium-high heat.
2. In a bowl, mix olive oil, lemon juice, garlic, thyme, salt, and pepper.
3. Toss squid rings in the marinade and let sit for 10 minutes.
4. Grill squid for 2–3 minutes per side, until charred and opaque.
5. Serve immediately, garnished with extra lemon wedges.

Fire-Grilled Bone Marrow
Ingredients:

- 4 beef marrow bones, cut lengthwise
- 2 tablespoons olive oil
- Salt and pepper to taste
- Fresh parsley, chopped (for garnish)
- Toasted baguette slices (for serving)

Instructions:

1. Preheat grill to medium-high heat.
2. Brush the marrow bones with olive oil, and season with salt and pepper.
3. Place bones on the grill, cut side up, and cook for 10–12 minutes, until the marrow is soft and begins to pull away from the bone.
4. Garnish with fresh parsley and serve with toasted baguette slices for spreading the marrow.

Charred Halloumi Skewers

Ingredients:

- 1 block of Halloumi cheese, cut into cubes
- 1 tablespoon olive oil
- 1 teaspoon dried oregano
- 1 teaspoon lemon zest
- Salt and pepper to taste
- Fresh lemon wedges for serving

Instructions:

1. Preheat grill to medium heat.
2. Thread the Halloumi cubes onto skewers, alternating with lemon wedges or other vegetables if desired.
3. Brush cheese with olive oil, and sprinkle with oregano, lemon zest, salt, and pepper.
4. Grill for 2–3 minutes per side until golden and charred.
5. Serve with extra lemon wedges.

Grilled Veal Chops with Rosemary Butter

Ingredients:

- 2 veal chops
- 2 tablespoons olive oil
- Salt and pepper to taste
- 2 tablespoons butter, melted
- 1 tablespoon fresh rosemary, finely chopped
- 1 clove garlic, minced

Instructions:

1. Preheat grill to medium-high heat.
2. Rub veal chops with olive oil, salt, and pepper.
3. Grill the chops for 4–5 minutes per side, or until they reach your preferred doneness.
4. In a small bowl, mix melted butter with rosemary and garlic.
5. Brush the veal chops with rosemary butter before serving.

Smoked Salmon Salad

Ingredients:

- 8 oz smoked salmon, torn into pieces
- 4 cups mixed salad greens (e.g., arugula, spinach, and lettuce)
- 1/2 red onion, thinly sliced
- 1 cucumber, sliced
- 1 tablespoon capers
- 1 tablespoon olive oil
- 1 tablespoon lemon juice
- Salt and pepper to taste

Instructions:

1. In a large bowl, combine the mixed greens, red onion, cucumber, and capers.
2. Gently toss in the smoked salmon pieces.
3. In a small bowl, whisk together olive oil, lemon juice, salt, and pepper to make a dressing.
4. Drizzle the dressing over the salad and toss gently.
5. Serve immediately as a light and refreshing appetizer or main.

Charred Sweet and Sour Chicken

Ingredients:

- 4 boneless chicken thighs
- 2 tablespoons olive oil
- 1/4 cup soy sauce
- 1/4 cup honey
- 2 tablespoons rice vinegar
- 1 tablespoon ketchup
- 1 garlic clove, minced
- 1 teaspoon fresh ginger, grated
- Salt and pepper to taste

Instructions:

1. Preheat grill to medium-high heat.
2. In a bowl, whisk together soy sauce, honey, rice vinegar, ketchup, garlic, ginger, salt, and pepper to create the marinade.
3. Place chicken thighs in a shallow dish and pour marinade over them. Let marinate for 30 minutes.
4. Grill the chicken for 6–8 minutes per side, brushing with the marinade as it cooks.
5. Serve with a drizzle of extra sauce and garnish with fresh herbs.

Fire-Roasted Beetroot Salad
 Ingredients:

- 4 medium beets, peeled and cut into wedges
- 1 tablespoon olive oil
- Salt and pepper to taste
- 2 tablespoons balsamic vinegar
- 1 tablespoon honey
- 2 cups arugula or mixed greens
- 1/4 cup goat cheese, crumbled (optional)

Instructions:

1. Preheat grill to medium-high heat.
2. Toss beetroot wedges with olive oil, salt, and pepper.
3. Grill beets for 4–5 minutes per side until charred and tender.
4. While the beets grill, whisk together balsamic vinegar and honey.
5. Toss the grilled beets with arugula and drizzle with balsamic-honey dressing.
6. Top with crumbled goat cheese if desired and serve warm.

Flame-Grilled Brisket Sliders

Ingredients:

- 1 lb smoked brisket, shredded
- 1 tablespoon barbecue sauce
- 8 slider buns
- 1/4 cup coleslaw
- Pickles for garnish

Instructions:

1. Preheat grill to medium heat.
2. Grill the slider buns for 1–2 minutes until lightly toasted.
3. In a saucepan, warm the shredded brisket with barbecue sauce.
4. Assemble sliders by placing a generous portion of brisket on each bun, topping with coleslaw and a pickle slice.
5. Serve these sliders hot for a delicious bite-sized meal.

Grilled Duck with Orange Glaze

Ingredients:

- 2 duck breasts
- 2 tablespoons olive oil
- Salt and pepper to taste
- 1/2 cup fresh orange juice
- 1 tablespoon honey
- 1 tablespoon soy sauce
- 1/2 teaspoon fresh thyme, chopped

Instructions:

1. Preheat grill to medium-high heat.
2. Rub duck breasts with olive oil, salt, and pepper.
3. Grill the duck for 4–5 minutes per side until the skin is crispy and the duck is medium-rare.
4. While the duck grills, make the glaze by simmering orange juice, honey, soy sauce, and thyme in a saucepan until it thickens (about 5 minutes).
5. Brush the duck with the glaze before serving, and garnish with extra thyme.

Wood-Fired Baked Alaska

Ingredients:

- 1 pre-made sponge cake or brownie base
- 2 cups vanilla ice cream
- 1 cup meringue (prepared with egg whites and sugar)
- 1 tablespoon dark rum (optional)

Instructions:

1. Preheat grill to medium-high heat or set up a wood fire.
2. Place the sponge cake or brownie base on a baking sheet and top with vanilla ice cream.
3. Cover the ice cream and cake completely with meringue.
4. Optionally, drizzle with dark rum for added flavor.
5. Carefully place the Baked Alaska on the grill for 2–3 minutes, just enough to brown the meringue (you can use a blow torch for an even better result).
6. Serve immediately and enjoy the warm, toasted meringue with the cold ice cream.

www.ingramcontent.com/pod-product-compliance
Lightning Source LLC
LaVergne TN
LVHW061951070526
838199LV00060B/4070